Discard

Bark & Tim

A True Story of Friendship
Based on the Paintings of Tim Brown

Audrey Glassman Vernick
Ellen Glassman Gidaro

The Overmountain Press

JOHNSON CITY, TENNESSEE

ISBN 1-57072-271-4

1 2 3 4 5 6 7 8 9 0

In memory of our mother, who believed in the magic of childhood and
filled our days with wonder and delight.
And for our families—the one we came from, and the ones we've grown.

Audrey and Ellen

For all my long-ago friends in the South,
many of whom are dead and gone.
And for those who like the stories they see in my paintings.

Tim

Life was very different when Tim Brown was a boy. In some ways, it was simpler. Where he lived, in the piney woods of Mississippi, children fished, climbed trees, and ran through the tall soft grass in the warm summer sun.

Tim played with Mama's cat some days, but what he really wanted was a dog. Mama said no.

Then the neighbor's dog, Mama Bark, had a sweet new puppy in the early-dark days between Halloween and Thanksgiving. Tim told Mama he needed to have that tiny puppy with its wiggly tail and its big-tooth smile. Mama still said no.

BARK FAMILY

BARK MAMA BARK

BABY BARK

JR

That Christmas Eve, like all the ones before, Papa brought home a fine tall tree. By bedtime, that tree shimmered like a winter sky. Tim hated saying good night to that beautiful tree, with its wintry pine smell.

CHRISTMAS TREE

But when it was time, Mama took Tim up to bed and tucked the warm blue blanket around him. His sleepy eyes closed, and he floated into the warm, cloudy mist of Christmas dreams.

A *krtch krtch krtch* sound woke Tim on Christmas morning. He'd never heard that sound before, and he followed it down the cold stairs and over to the tree. There, beneath the sparkly branches, was a big box topped with a fancy red bow.

The box was making the *krtch* sound! When Tim untied the ribbon, the box shook and jumped and tipped. Out jumped Baby Bark.

"He's all yours," Papa said.

"Merry Christmas," said Mama.

Tim's sister thought Bark looked scary. She didn't like his big, pointy teeth. But Tim knew that Bark was gentle, even if his smile was a little toothy.

When Tim's sister got to know Bark, she realized he was a sweet puppy. She still wished he had normal teeth, though. And a fancy dog's curly fur.

But Bark was a mutt and Tim loved him. He was the best dog ever.

PAINTING MY FAMILY TB

After Bark, what Tim loved best was painting. He painted for the joy of it. And when he was done, after he washed the reds, yellows, and blues from his brushes, Bark was always waiting.

TB KITE FLYING WITH FAMILY

When Tim sat under a tree, Bark was with him. When Tim napped in the hammock, Bark lay right beside him. And when Tim's family flew their kite in the windy sky above the hill, Bark bounded right along, jumping high to catch the kite's swirling tail in his mouth.

Sometimes Bark made up his own games.
"Chase Mama's Cat" was his favorite.

Tim tried to help Bark be good, but that dog loved mischief! Papa didn't mind too much, but it seemed like every day, Bark found a different way to make Mama mad. She was always chasing Bark with her scratchy broom.

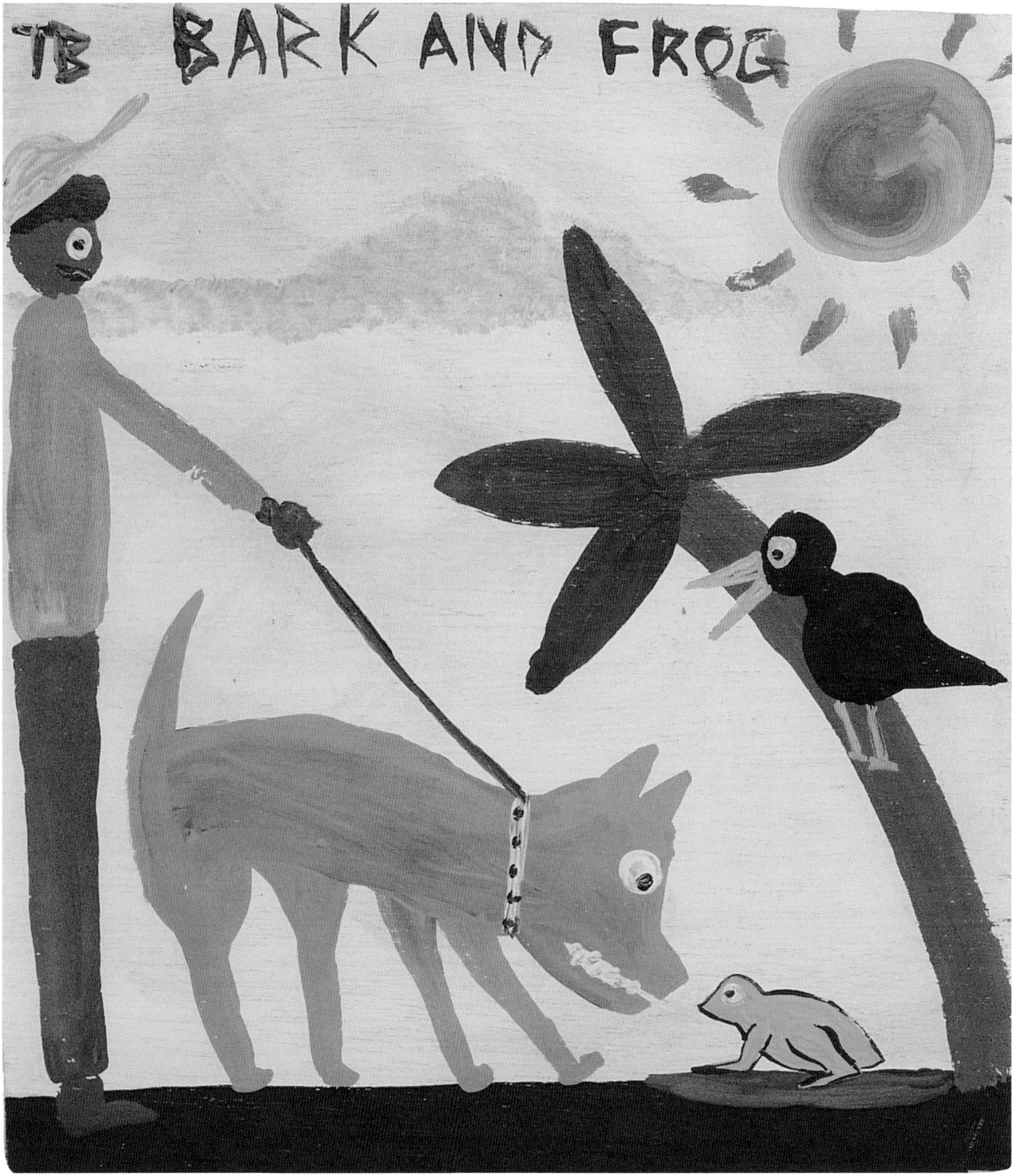
TB BARK AND FROG

Tim and Bark decided it would be smart to stay out of Mama's way when she was cross. Sometimes Tim would grab his paints, and they'd go off to find a peaceful spot to sit. Other times, they took long walks together, stopping to say hey to any friends that walked, flew, or hopped across their trail.

In the spring, when the air smelled sweet and the ground felt squishy, Bark just had to roll in the cool, shiny mud. Tim laughed at the sounds he made. *Sploch! Glurp! Blurgh!* He loved how Bark's paws pointed up toward the setting sun.

"You are one sruffy-looking dog," Tim always told him.

TB SRUFFY BARK

TB WASHING BARK

When the sun slipped down low in the sky, Tim would start toward home, and Bark would soon follow. But he'd follow very slowly. As soon as he saw the tub in the yard, he'd dig his paws deep into the ground. Bark hated baths. Every time Tim put him in the water, Bark would try to jump out. Tim had to keep wrestling Bark's wet dog body right back into the tub.

Tim took such good care of Bark. That dog's life was full! He loved running and swimming and chasing cats and birds. He loved rubbing his back on the bumpy trunk of the red oak and lifting his nose to sniff after a soaking rain. But more than anything, more than anything else in the world, that dog loved his friend Tim.

From summer to winter and back again, Bark and Tim played together—for years and years, until they were much, much older.

Tim always knew that dogs don't live as long as people, but when Bark died, Tim missed him. He was so sad to lose his friend. He hoped the angels in heaven would sit with Bark and nap beside him. He hoped that if they flew a bright white kite, they would let Bark lead the way.

Tim had other dogs after Bark. Some could do tricks and most listened to him better. None of them knew how to get Mama hopping mad, and none of them grabbed Tim's hat the way Bark had. But Bark was Tim's favorite. He loved him the most. He never stopped thinking about Bark. He never stopped loving him.

Tim also never stopped painting. He has painted hundreds of pictures, and his old friend Bark is in many of them. Tim's paintings have been seen by people near his home and far, far away.

And now these people think about Bark a lot, too. They imagine what it would be like to have a great dog like Bark, and they think about how lucky Bark was to have a friend like Tim.

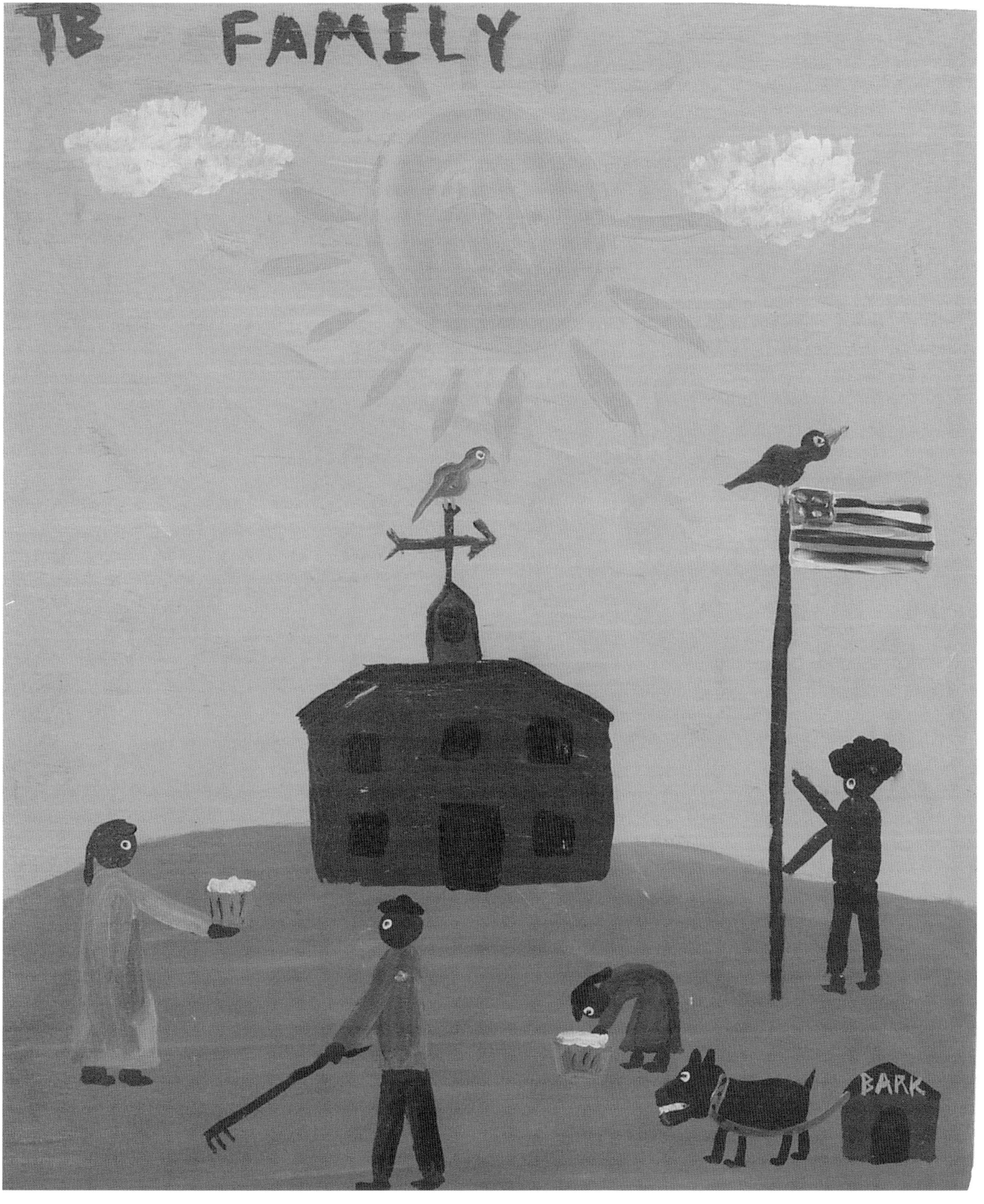
TB
FAMILY
BARK

Artist Tim Brown

Tim Brown was born on August 4, 1924. He lived with his parents and his little sister, Annie, in a house near Jackson, Mississippi.

I grew up in the house I was born in. My papa was Timmy, but Mama called him Papa Bull. My mama was Thelma, but Papa called her Honey.

My sister was two years younger than me. She was mean to me sometimes, but we had fun.

Every day was like Christmas and Thanksgiving because our family was always together for dinner.

Tim's family grew vegetables and raised cows and pigs. His grandparents and aunt lived right next door. There were no other children living nearby, so Tim and his sister played together a lot.

We played jacks and jump rope. Sometimes I slept in the same room with my sister, but on hot summer nights, I slept outside in the barn. I also slept in my room, but it was small.

We had a small house. We painted it different colors often because we had a lot of house paint. We painted it blue one time, and also yellow, and red other times.

The land beyond that little painted house was loud with animal sounds.

I had many dogs. I had Bark, Spot, and Snowball. Mama's cat was named Spike. I had a crow once.

I saw deer and turtles and possums. I saw alligators. I hunted for those and we ate them.

Tim and his family ate food they caught or grew themselves. They worked in the fields, picking vegetables and cotton. Sometimes Tim helped his father do construction work.

My papa worked so hard in the field. My mama and papa were fine. My mama was nice, but when she got mad, she was strict. My papa was a good man. He took care of us.

Sometimes Tim's papa got mad, like when Tim used his house paint to create his first pictures. Tim doesn't remember his very first painting, but he remembers some of the ones he did when he was little.

I painted things that were happening in my life. My mama and papa liked my paintings. My sister thought my paintings were stupid.

In addition to painting, swimming and fishing were Tim's favorite things to do. Sometimes, the circus, magicians, and musicians would travel through town, but most of Tim's best memories are simple and quiet.

Sometimes in the spring we went to the big river and we went to the ocean beach, but most of the time we stayed at home and went fishing and swimming. My favorite times were hot summer nights and watching the stars and outside cookouts.

In the fall, Tim and Annie went to school. Tim attended school until he was sixteen. He volunteered to join the Army when he was nineteen.

I went to California and stayed there for four years. Sometimes I went on a ship.

After the Army, Tim tried to live outside Mississippi, but he was always drawn back home. He was always drawn back to painting, too. He got married in 1950 and had two children. It wasn't until his children had grown that Tim sold his first painting. Since then he has sold more than a thousand paintings.

Before he actually takes his brushes out, Tim spends a long time imagining what the painting will be.

Sometimes I think for a month before I paint. I usually think about how I was when I was a child and I try to paint that. Sometimes I think about crazy things that I wanted to do when I was a child or something that happened, and I make it a little more than it really was, but usually I paint what really happened.

Tim still lives in Mississippi. He likes to remember his childhood days, his family, Bark, and all the fun they shared.

I relax a lot. I still grow some vegetables. I go fishing sometimes.

I waited a long time for the world to see my artwork. Now I hope people will look at my paintings and think about how life was for a young black child growing up in the 1920s and 1930s. It was a fun life but also hard.

The background painting is a self-portrait of Tim Brown.

Authors Audrey and Ellen

Audrey and Ellen grew up in Queens, New York, with their parents and their sister, Beth. Ellen is the oldest of the three girls; Audrey is the youngest. Their childhood memories include backyard carnivals, punchball games, ice cream trucks, and dramatic productions in their garage.

Ellen went on to study journalism and graduated from New York University. After a decade of writing and editing college publications, she began a family. Ellen lives with her husband and their three sons in Wynnewood, Pennsylvania.

Her love for children's literature found its place in Ellen's second career as an elementary-school teacher. She currently teaches second grade at a public school in Swarthmore, Pennsylvania.

Audrey writes for children and adults. She has published short fiction in literary and commercial magazines. Her nonfiction book, *Can I Fax a Thank-You Note*, was published by Berkley in 1998. She received an MFA in creative writing from Sarah Lawrence College in 1992 and a fiction fellowship from the New Jersey State Council on the Arts in 1999.

She lives near the ocean in New Jersey with her husband, son, and daughter.

The Bark & Tim Story

We came across a painting, *Feeding Bark*, for sale on eBay. There was something so sweet, simple, and moving about this painting that we kept coming back to it. It seemed like that painting had a story to tell.

Once we hatched the idea to write about Bark and Tim, we imagined traveling to Mississippi to interview Tim about his childhood. We soon learned, through his manager, that Tim insists on maintaining absolute privacy. He prefers to be interviewed through the mail. We also learned, from a series of back-and-forth questions, that he is a self-taught artist who began painting because he had no photographs from his childhood, and he wanted to share his memories.

It is our great honor to share his pictures through this book. Although we probably will never meet him, we feel as though we share a strong bond with this man, whose artwork touches us so deeply.

Audrey Glassman Vernick and Ellen Glassman Gidaro, July 2003

"No matter how little money and how few possessions you own, having a dog makes you rich."

John Steinbeck

Tim's Paintings

In the broadest sense of the term, Tim's work is defined as folk art. Some, however, feel his work is better categorized as "outsider" art or "visionary" art. We have listed a few definitions below, as well as information about where you can further research art like Tim's.

From the National Endowment for the Arts: Folk & Traditional Arts are those that are learned as part of the cultural life of a community whose members share a common ethnic heritage, language, religion, occupation, or geographic region. These traditions are shaped by the aesthetics and values of a shared culture and are passed from generation to generation, most often within family and community through observation, conversation, and practice.

From the American Folk Art Museum: In the United States, the term *folk art* refers to a diverse range of visual expressions, including paintings, sculpture, textiles, and pottery, created by artists and artisans whose skills were obtained through a variety of means outside academic training in the arts. Folk art is often inspired by shared cultural heritage, community traditions, patriotism, religion, and popular culture. It may serve utilitarian needs or express individual beliefs. Some of folk art's many embracing forms are made from everyday materials and serve everyday needs, such as quilts, coverlets, samplers, hooked rugs, weathervanes, whirligigs, gravestones, decoys, painted signs, portraits, landscapes, and seascapes. Contemporary expressions by self-taught artists may be fashioned from traditional art-making mediums or salvaged materials that have been transformed into aesthetic objects with meaning for their creators. Folk art is an important part of American culture, a material reflection of significant themes and trends in American life.

From the American Visionary Art Museum: Visionary art as defined for the purposes of the American Visionary Art Museum refers to art produced by self-taught individuals, usually without formal training, whose works arise from an innate personal vision that revels foremost in the creative act itself.

To see more of Tim Brown's work, visit on the Web: http://www.worldoffolkart.com/timbrown.htm

Parents: Folk art draws from a wide range of subjects. With that in mind, you might want to take a look at the art before sending your children to this Web site.

Special thanks to:

National Endowment for the Arts
1100 Pennsylvania Avenue NW
Washington, DC 20506
202-682-5400
www.nea.gov

American Folk Art Museum
45 West 53rd Street
New York, NY 10019
212-265-1040
www.folkartmuseum.org

American Visionary Art Museum
800 Key Highway
Baltimore, MD 21230
410-244-1900
www.avam.org